333

ORIGAMI
SHEETS

ASTROMAGIC DESIGNS

High-Quality Double-Sided Paper Pack Book

C&T PUBLISHING
Another Maker Inspired!

Introduction

Magically beautiful patterns meet traditional folding fun!
"Origami" is a very old paper folding technique that
originated in Asia. For a long time it was an integral part
of religious ceremonies, and in Japan the folded crane is
still considered a symbol of good luck. Your creations will
look amazing in the various cosmo-themed patterns. This
book will help you to fold your own magnificent animals
and other figures quickly and easily.

On the following pages, you will find a selection of folding
instructions that you can use to make some impressive
origami pieces. With these 333 patterned papers, there
are endless combinations and folding possibilities.

Happy folding!

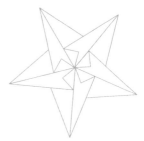

BASIC SHAPE: KITE

1. To make a diagonal fold, position the paper so that one corner is facing you. Take the corner and fold it over to meet the opposite corner. Make a crease and then unfold the sheet.

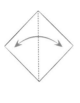

2. Fold the outer edges of the paper inward to line up with the diagonal crease you have just made.

INSIDE REVERSE FOLD

1. Fold the tip inward and then unfold.

2. Gently pull the sides outward and fold the point down (between the sides).

 Finished!

The kite is the basic shape for many **stars**.

 Finished!

The inside reverse fold is used to form the head of bird figures, such as the **dove** and **crane**.

Dove

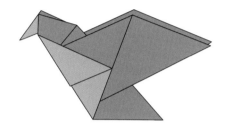

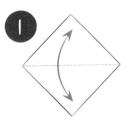

Make a diagonal fold by placing two opposite corners on top of each other and then unfold the sheet.

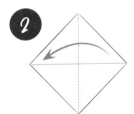

Make a second diagonal fold with the other two corners, but do not unfold the sheet when you are done.

Take the tip of the triangle and fold about two-thirds of it to the right so that it slightly overlaps the long edge.

Open up the triangle by taking the top layer and folding about two-thirds of it to the left.

Fold the top half of the shape down so that the top corner lines up with the bottom corner.

Now fold the "wings" up.

Make the head using an inside reverse fold.

Finished!

Now your dove is ready to take flight. Whether as a gift or as a bringer of peace—with such a magical pattern it lives up to its meaning!

Snake

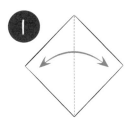

1

Make a diagonal fold by placing two opposite corners on top of each other, then unfold the sheet.

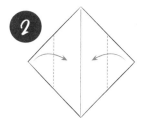

2

Fold the outer corners in toward the center.

3

Fold the outside edges in again toward the center.

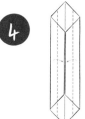

4

Fold the sides in once more.

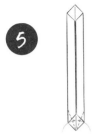

5

Fold the bottom corner up toward the center.

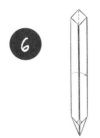

6

Fold the shape in half vertically.

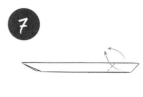

7

Fold the front section upward to make an outside reverse fold for the neck.

8

Make another outside reverse fold for the head.

9

Make alternating inward and outward folds for the snake's body.

Finished!

Gift

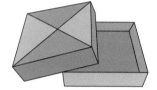

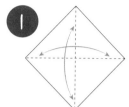

1 First fold the left corner onto the right corner and back again. Then fold the bottom corner onto the top corner and back again.

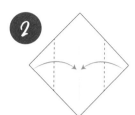

2 Fold the left and right corners to the center of the paper.

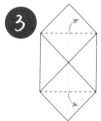

3 Now fold the top and bottom corners to the center—but towards the back!

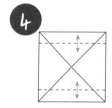

4 Fold the top edge down and back again. The fold line should be about a third of the way down the top half of the sheet. Do the same with the bottom edge.

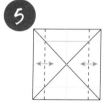

5 Repeat Step 4 for the left and right outer edges as well.

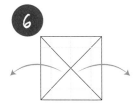

Fold the left and right corners outwards again.

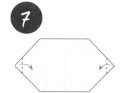

Now fold the left and right corners to the outermost fold line on each side.

Fold the left and right outer corners again to the next fold line towards the middle.

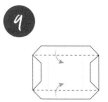

Fold the top and bottom edges towards the middle along the existing fold line so that they stand vertically upwards.

Fold the right outer edge vertically upwards at the second fold line from the outside. Fold the top half down over the tabs on the sides. Repeat with the left side.

Finished!

So that the lid will later fit on the lower part of the box, take new paper for the lower part and cut off a 3/16″ (0.5cm) wide strip on each side. Then repeat all steps in these instructions.

Dragon

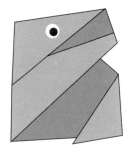

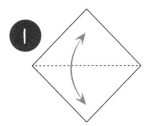

1 Fold the top corner onto the bottom corner and back again to create a center line.

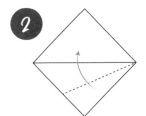

2 Fold the bottom right edge to the center line.

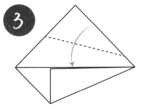

3 Now fold the right top edge down along the dashed line.

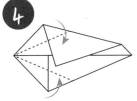

4 Then fold the left upper and lower outer edges to the center line.

5

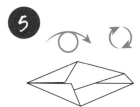

Smooth out the folds. Turn your model over and rotate it a little counterclockwise.

6

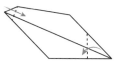

Fold the left corner to the right as shown and then fold the right corner slightly to the left.

7

Then fold the left area to the right along the dashed line.

8

Just paint one eye and the little dragon is ready!

 Finished!

Crane

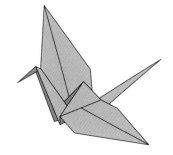

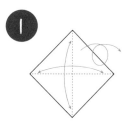

Make two diagonal folds, then unfold the sheet and turn it over.

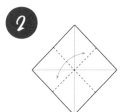

Fold the two parallel diagonals and unfold the sheet again.

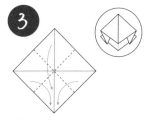

Place a finger on the center of the sheet so that the sides start to fold up. Now push the prefolded shape together.

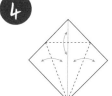

Position the folded shape in front of you so that the open tip is facing you. Fold the left and right edges in toward the central crease, then fold the top corner down.

Fold the bottom corner upward and the outer edges will automatically move to the center.

Turn the shape over and fold the bottom corner up as in the previous step.

 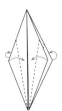

Fold the left and right corners toward the center. Turn the shape over again and repeat the process on the other side.

Use two inside reverse folds to make the crane's tail and neck.

Now make the head using one inside reverse fold, and fold the wings out to the sides.

 Finished!

In Japan, cranes are the symbol of a happy life. Legend also says that if you make 1,000 origami cranes, you can make a wish. So go ahead—your crane will be really glad to have some company.

Star Wreath

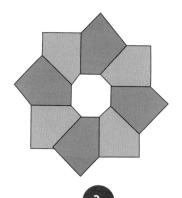

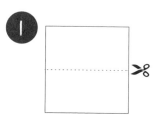

For this little star you first have to cut 4 square sheets in half. This will give you 8 rectangles.

Then fold a rectangle upwards as shown.

Then fold the left and right corners down.

Finally, fold the piece in half to the right.

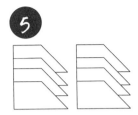

5

Repeat this with the other rectangles until all 8 pieces are finished.

6

On the short, straight edge of the first star point, slide the tip of the second point between the two outer pockets.

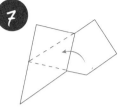

7

Push the second point firmly in as shown.

Finished!

When you have put all the pieces together, push the last tip into the pockets of the first wing, thus closing your wreath of stars. Many different wreaths create a pretty star decoration.

Starlet

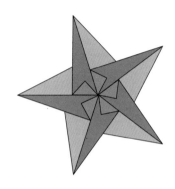

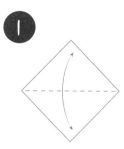

Fold the bottom corner onto the top corner and back again.

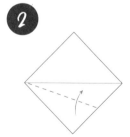

Fold the bottom left edge to the center line.

Your fold will now look like the one shown above.

Now fold the bottom part up.

Now fold the right tip to the left and back again as shown.

Then fold the right tip upwards as shown.

Then fold the entire small triangle to the left.

It looks like this. You need five equal parts for your star.

Now glue the 5 parts together.

 Finished!

In the end you have to glue the last star point to the first point. This creates a little star that looks lovely on a Christmas card.

Stargazer

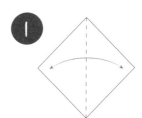

1

Fold the right corner onto the left corner and back again.

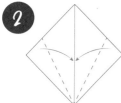

2

Fold the two bottom edges to the center line. You will now have a kite.

3

Then fold the left and right edges again to the center line.

4

Your kite is now a little narrower. Turn your model over.

5

You will need 8 points for the finished star.

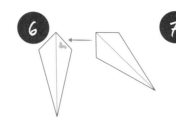

6

Now put some glue on your first point as shown to stick the second point in place.

7

The inside tips of the points are on top of each other and the short edge aligns, as shown, on the previous point's center line.

8

Once all 8 wings have been glued together, connect the last and first points together.

✓ Finished!

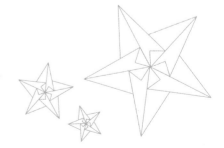

Sunstar

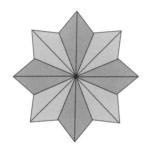

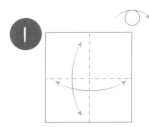

1 Fold the bottom edge onto the top edge and back again. Then fold the right edge to the left edge and back again.

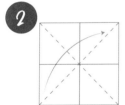

2 Fold all the tips together and back again.

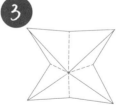

3 Now push the right and left outer edges inwards and fold the triangle down.

4 Your model now looks like this from the front.

Now press the model flat on all edges.

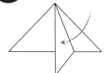

Now fold one of the right edges to the center line.

Then fold one of the left edges to the center line. This is now a finished point. You need 8 of these.

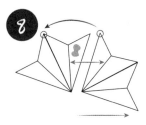

Now you can glue the first two points together. The inside tips lie together. At the top, overlap the points together as shown.

Glue all the points together like this.

Finished!

At the end, glue the last point to the first point. This is how a three-dimensional star is created.

Little Star

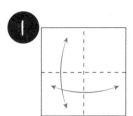

Fold the bottom edge onto the top edge and back again. Then the right edge to the left edge and back again.

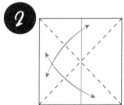

Then fold all the tips together and back again.

Place the paper in front of you with the point facing up and fold the bottom point to the center point.

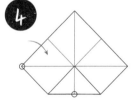

Now fold the left tip to the middle of the bottom edge (see marked circles).

It should look like this. But only crease the bottom half up to the fold line you made in Step 1.

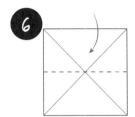

Then unfold the entire paper again. Then fold the top edge onto the bottom edge.

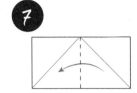

And then the right edge to the left edge.

You will receive a small square with two crossed fold lines.

Now open the top, pull the left tip over to the right side and press the new triangle down.

Then turn your model over and repeat the process with the other side.

Now you have a triangle. Now fold the right edge to the center line.

Turn the model over and fold the right edge to the center line here too.

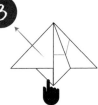

Now hold the lower left tip and the right point with your fingers and pull the left point outwards.

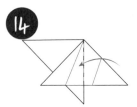

Then fold the right wing to the left.

You will now see a small fold line you made in Step 5. Fold so the side of the right point lines up with that fold line.

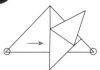

Then fold the left point to the right. The tips marked with circles lie on top of each other.

17

Now fold the same point over to the left as shown.

18

The new point should now form a line with the right point.

19

Then turn your model over and the star is finished.

Finished!

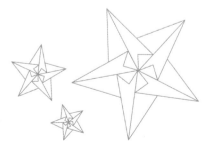

333 Origami Sheets AstroMagic Designs

First published in the United States in 2024 by C&T Publishing, Inc., P.O. Box 1456, Lafayette, CA 94549

EMF © Edition Michael Fischer GmbH, 2023

www.emf-verlag.de

This edition of "333 ORIGAMI – ASTRO MAGIC" first published in Germany by Edition Michael Fischer GmbH in 2023 is published by arrangement with Silke Bruenink Agency, Munich, Germany.

PUBLISHER: Amy Barrett-Daffin

CREATIVE DIRECTOR: Gailen Runge

SENIOR ACQUISITIONS EDITOR: Roxane Cerda

PRODUCT MANAGER: Betsy La Honta

ENGLISH-LANGUAGE COVER DESIGNER: April Mostek

ENGLISH TRANSLATION: Krista Hold and Gailen Runge

PRODUCTION COORDINATOR: Zinnia Heinzmann

Instructions and folding symbols dove, snake, gift: EMF; Crane: © tofang/Shutterstock; Dragon: Thade Precht

Instructions star wreath, starlet, stargazer, sunstar, small star: Ina Mielkau Folding symbols star wreath, starlet, stargazer, sunstar, small star: Thade Precht

Images from Shutterstock:

Pattern gold: © Tanya Antusenok; © lyubava.21; © coldsun777; © Valedi; © lyubava.21; © lyubava.21; © Merfin; © Valedi

pattern beige: © lyubava.21; © Anastasia_Panchenko; © Lucky Project; © lyubava.21; © Sunnydream; © lyubava.21; © Mio Buono; © Dimec

pattern lilac: © Elonalaff; © Sunnydream; © Anna Holyph; © Melok; © Svetolk; © Anastasiia Vasylyk; © Tanya Antusenok; © Anastasia_Panchenko

Pattern midnight blue: © xenia_ok; © Rolau Elena; © meow_meow; © Valedi; © Transia Design; © YuHusar; © lyubava.21; © In-Finity

pattern blue: © ONYXprj; © Kjpargeter; © Gorbash Varvara; © miumi; © Chikovnaya; © Inge Randma; © Diana Kovach; © Merfin

Printed in China

10 9 8 7 6 5 4 3 2 1

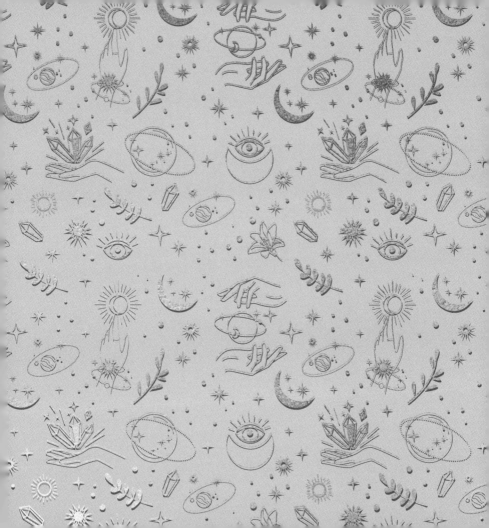

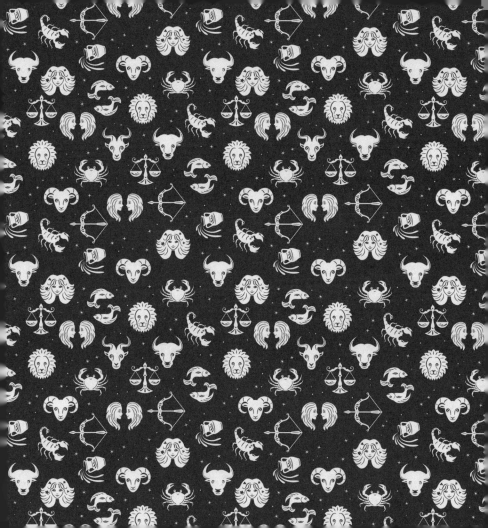

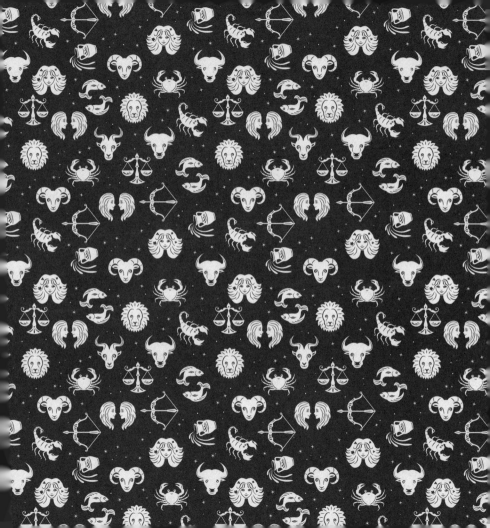

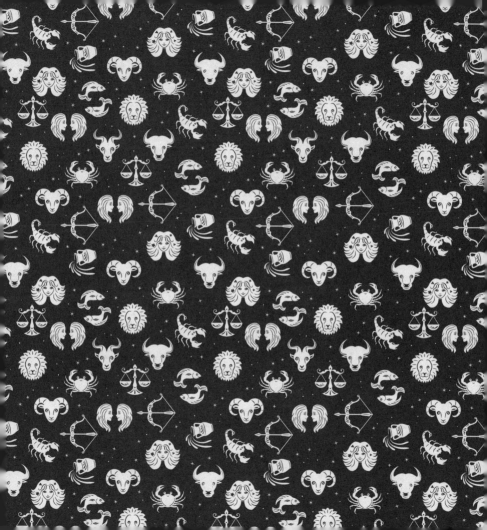

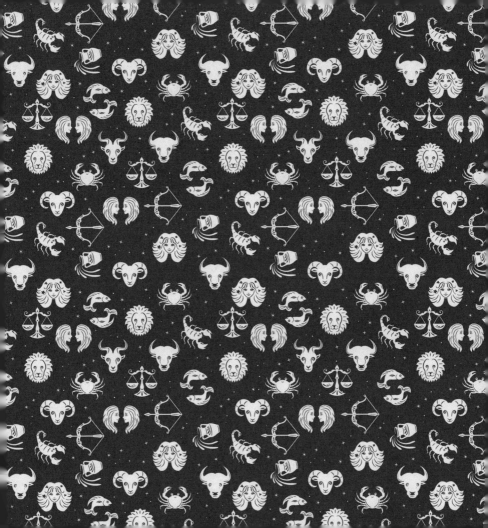

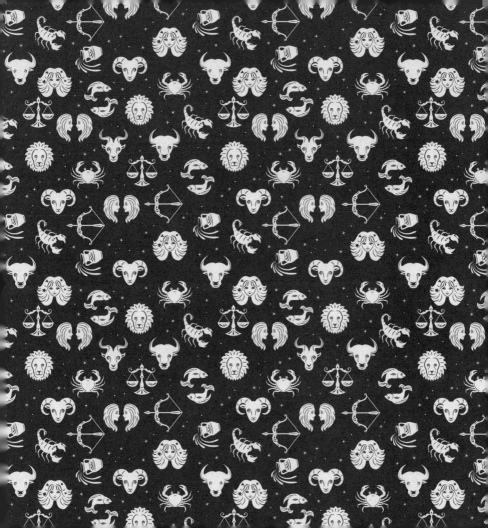

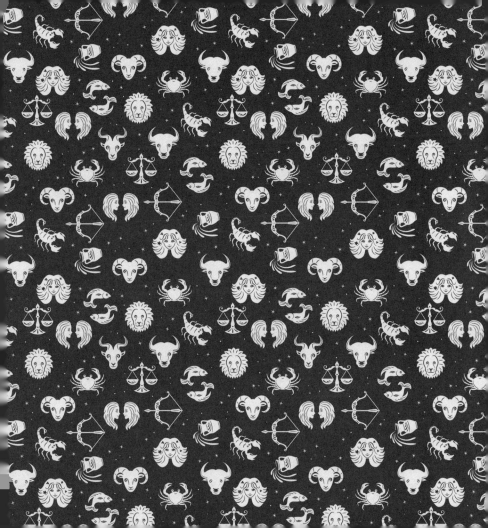

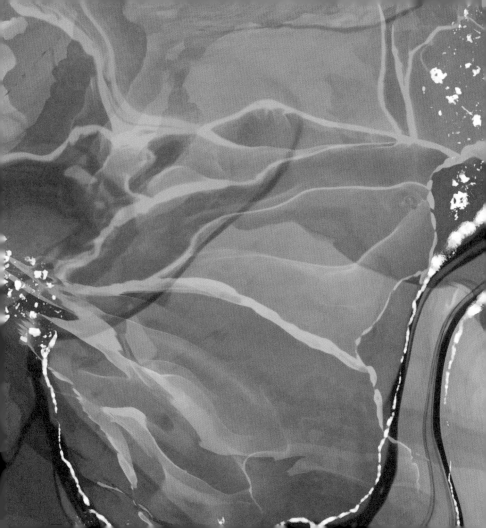

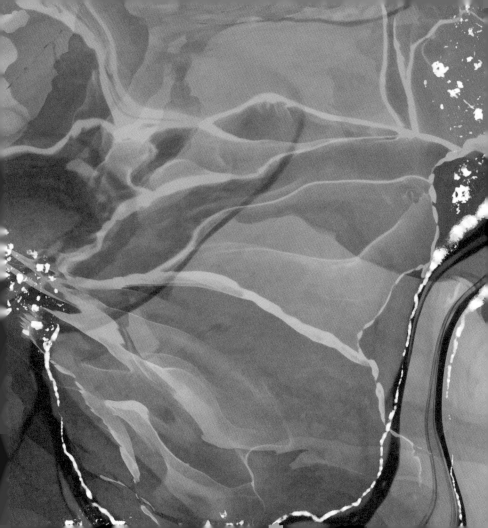

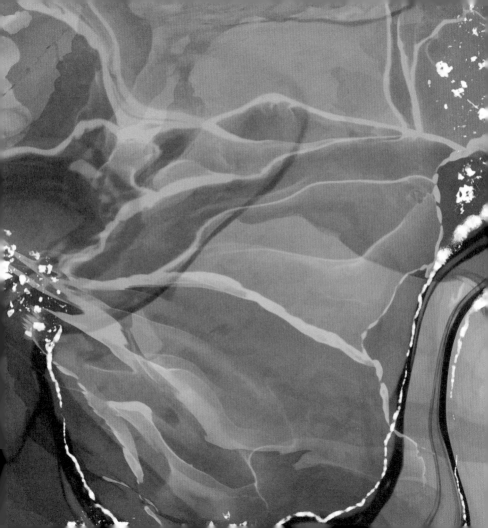

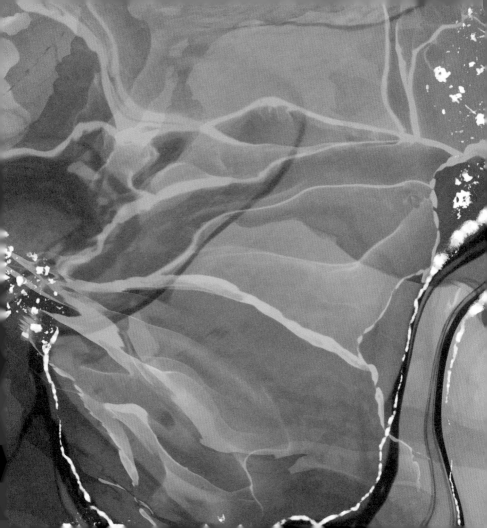

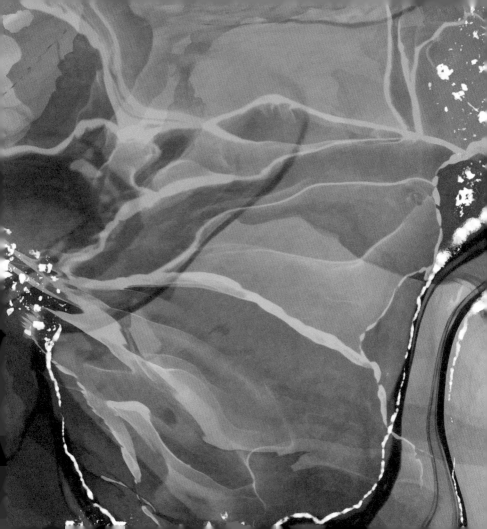

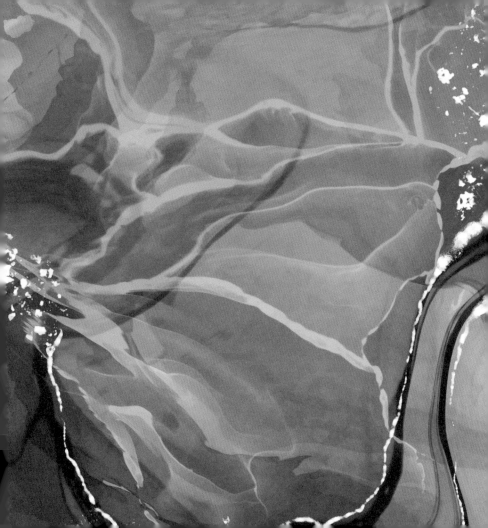

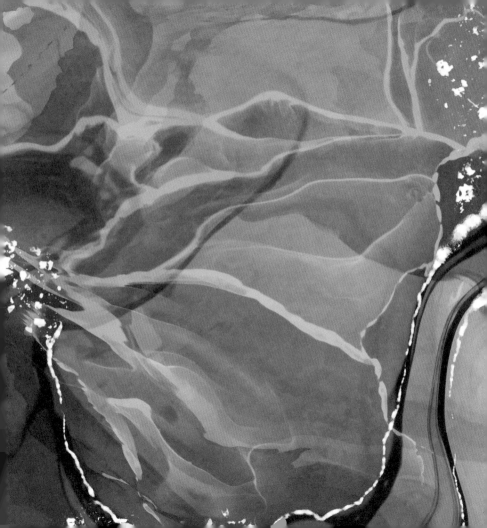

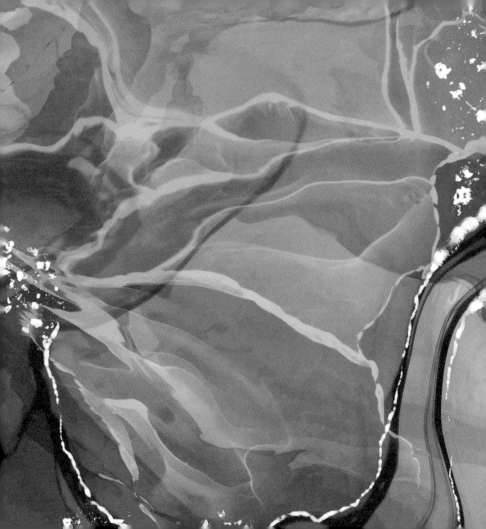

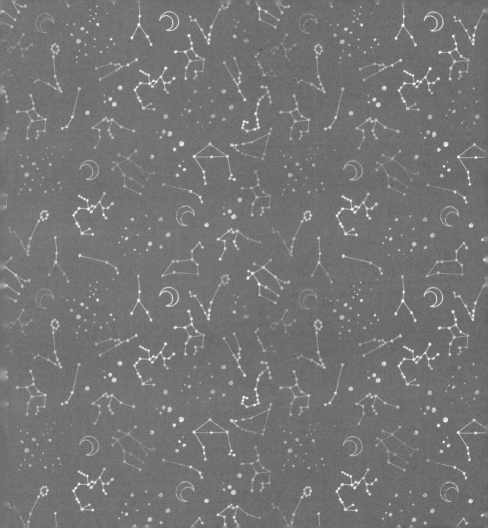

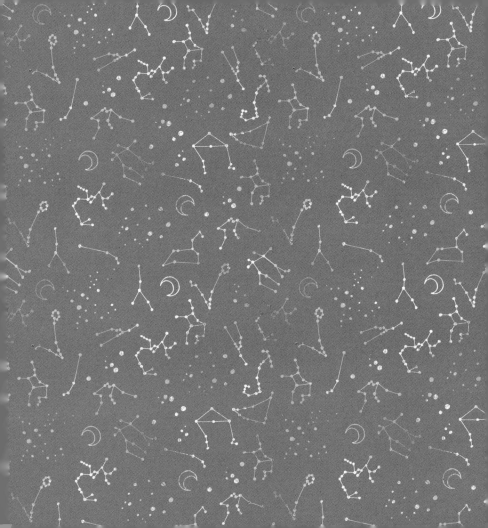

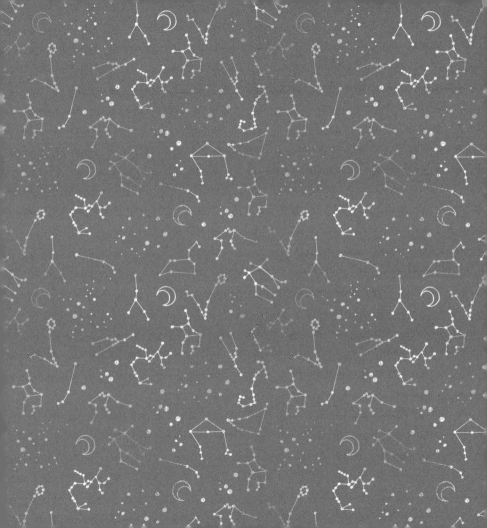

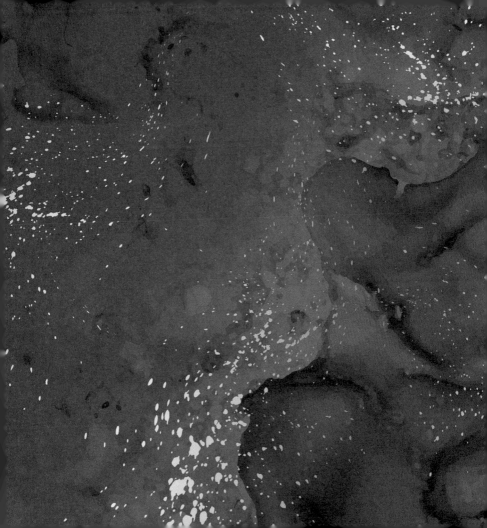

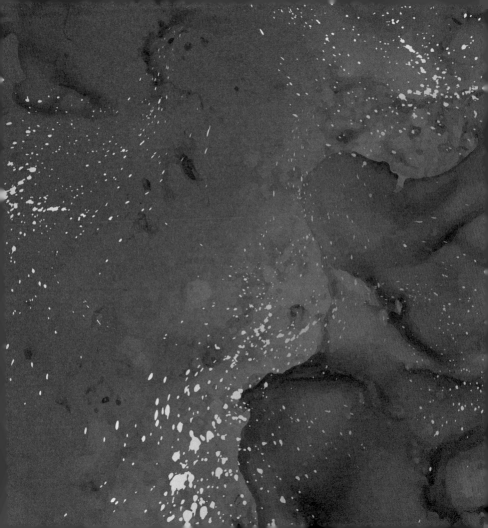

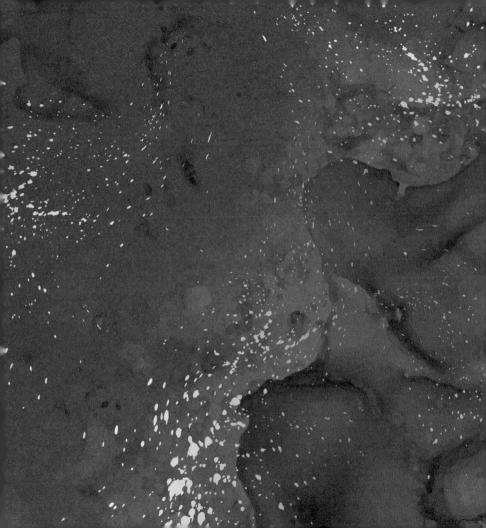

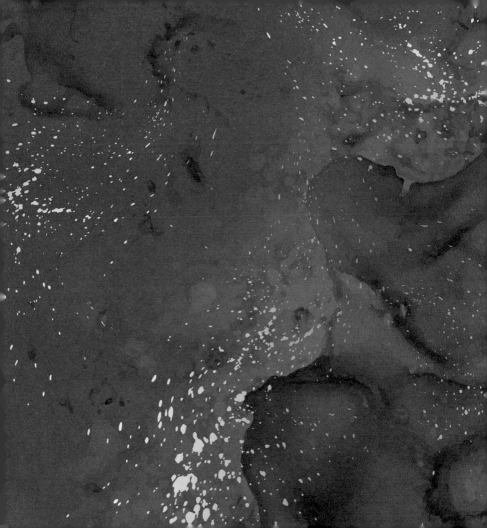

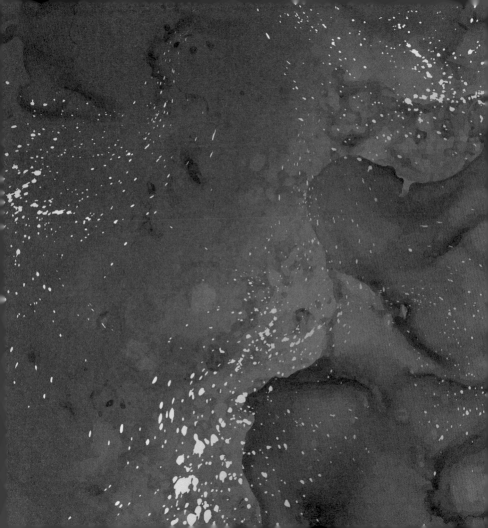

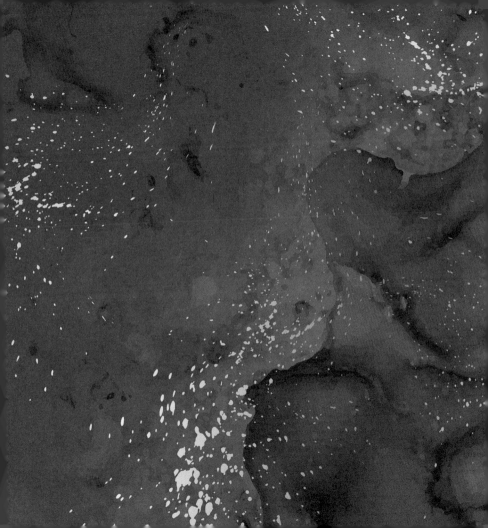

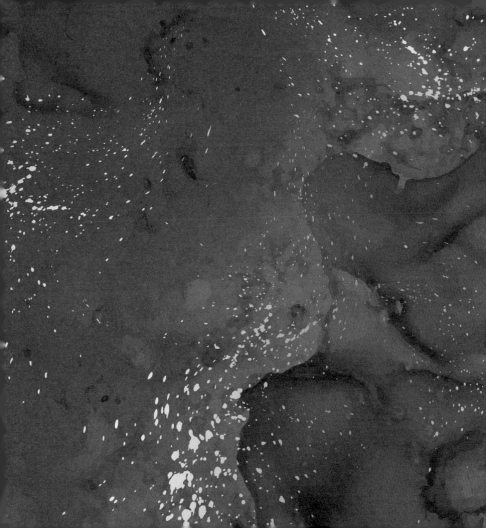

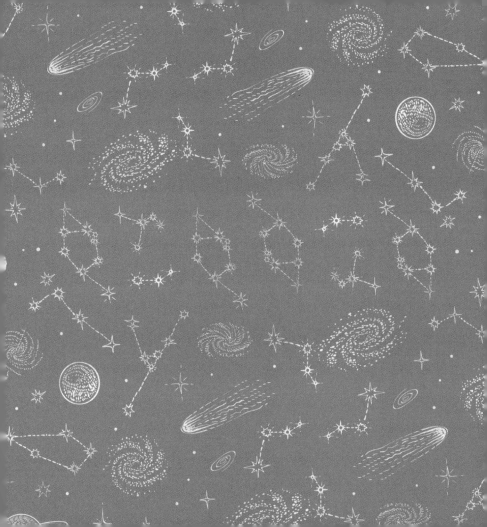

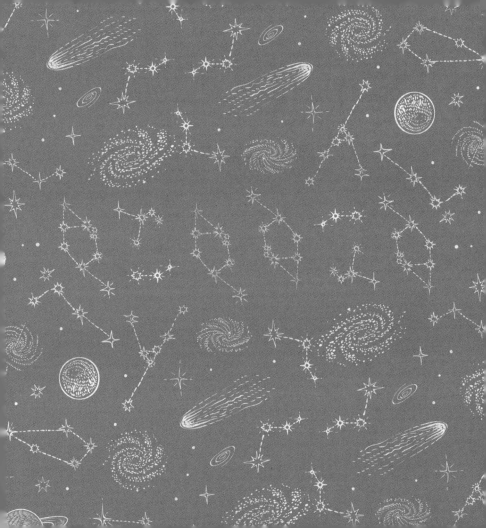

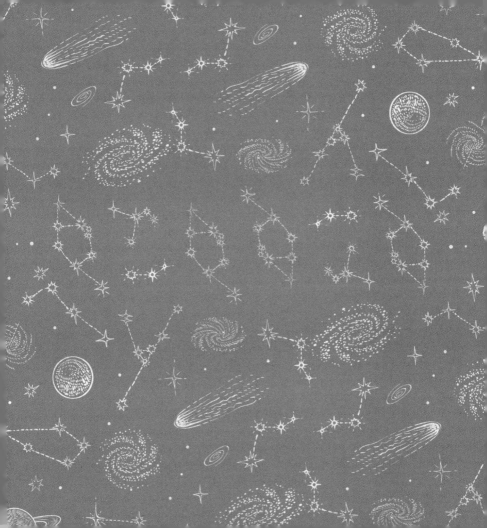

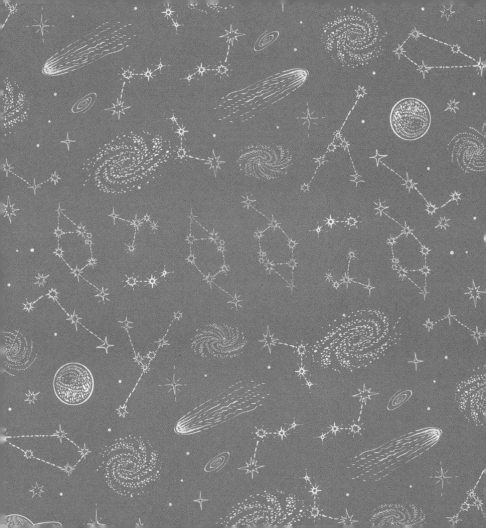

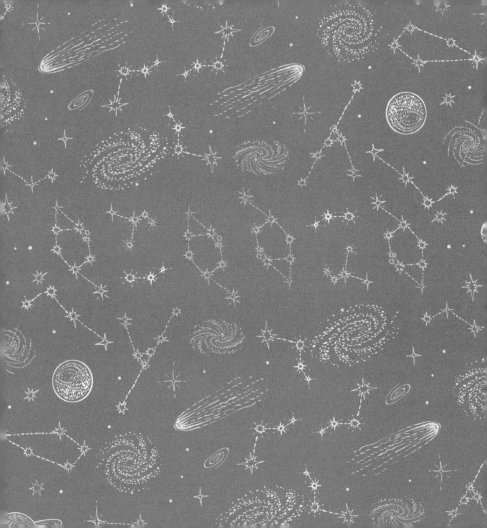

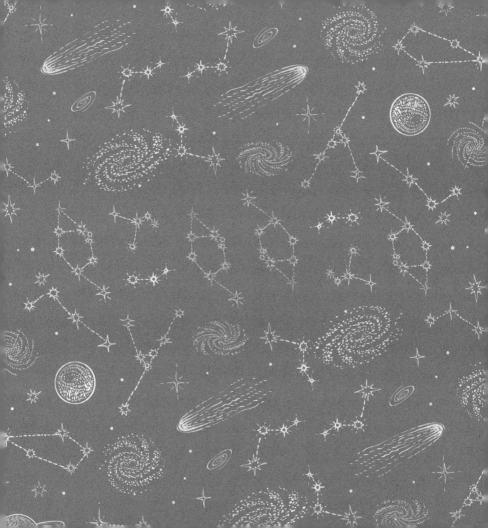

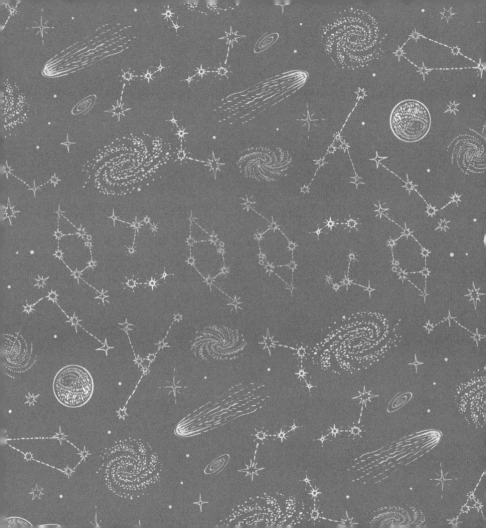

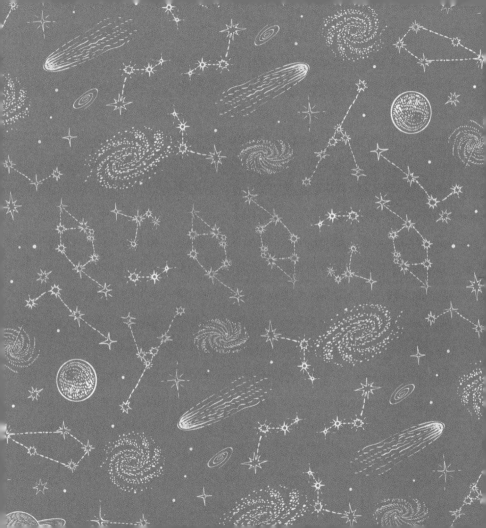

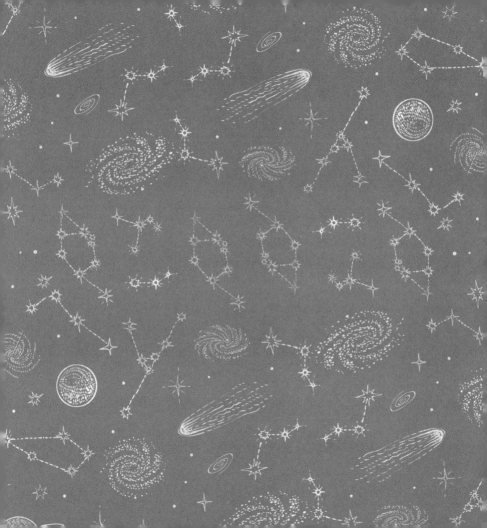

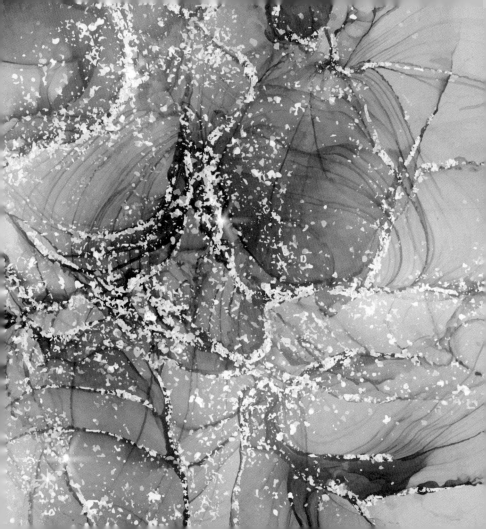

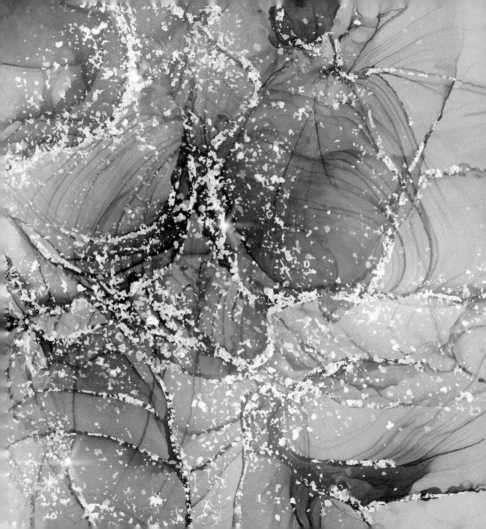

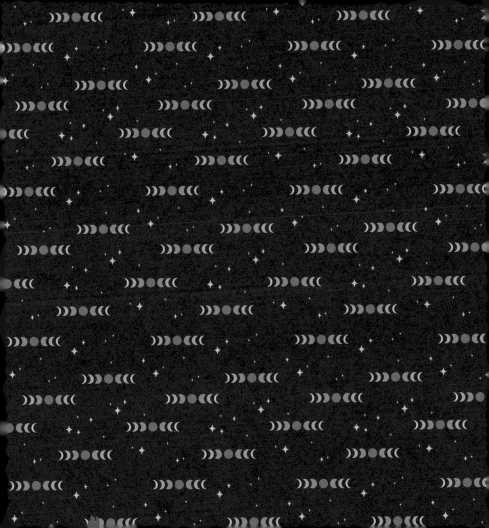

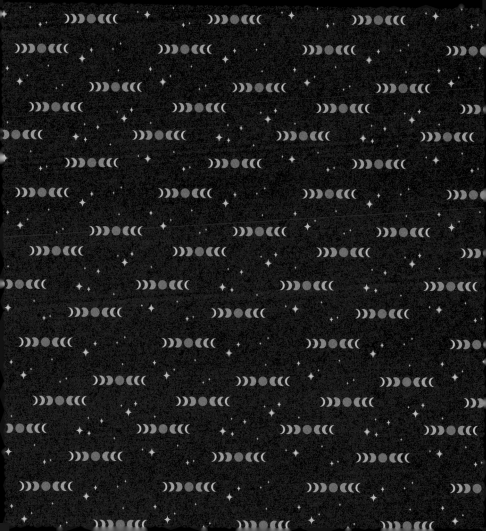

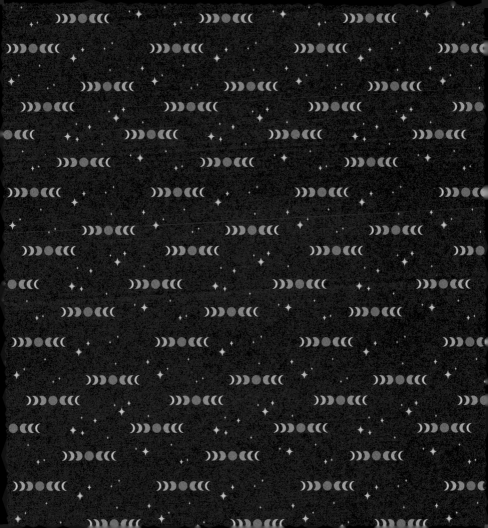

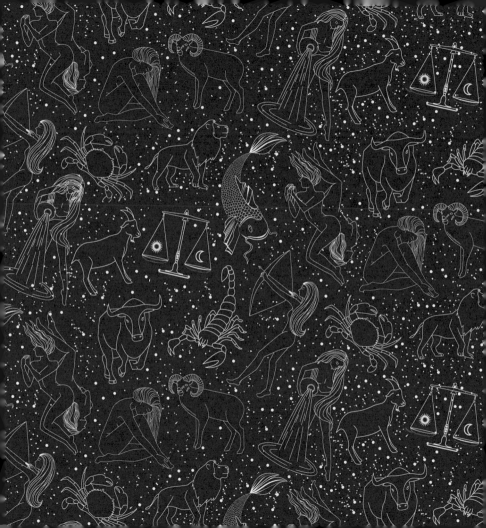

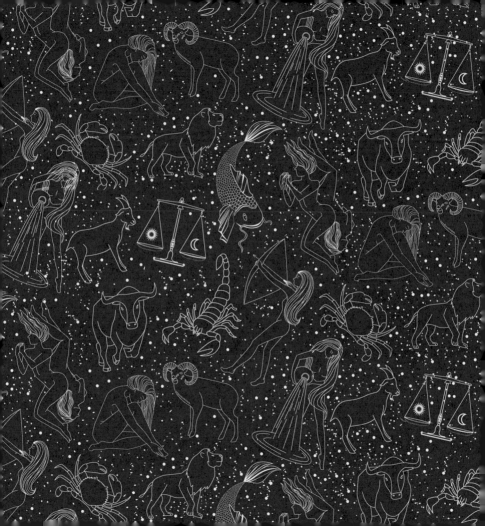

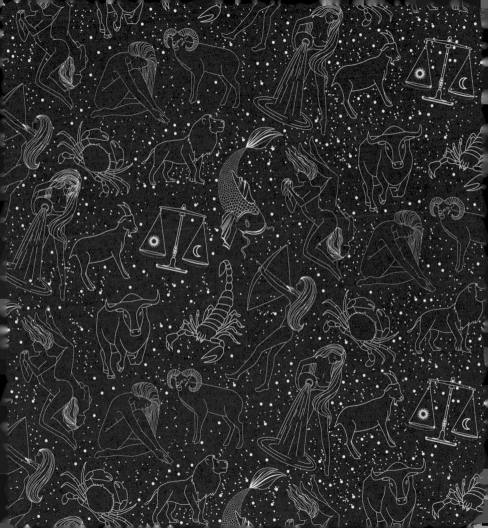

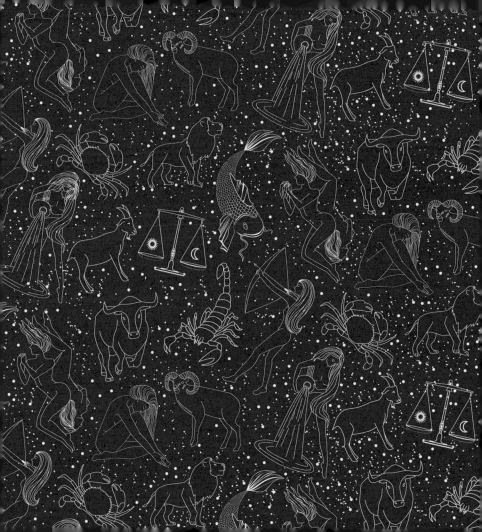

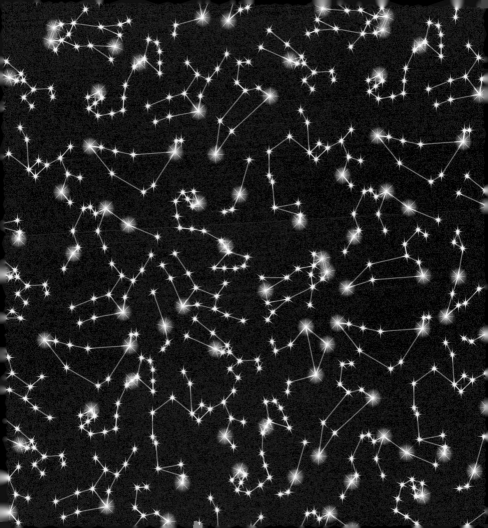

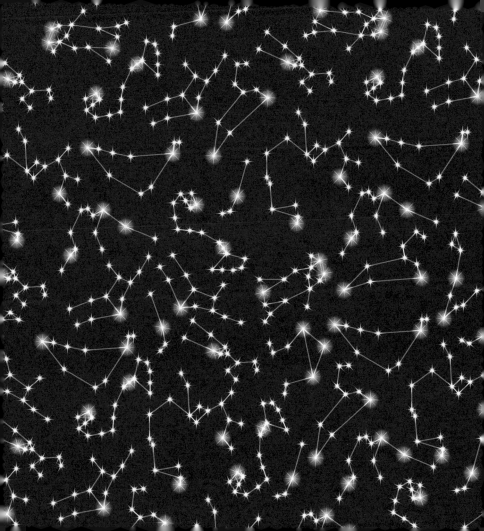

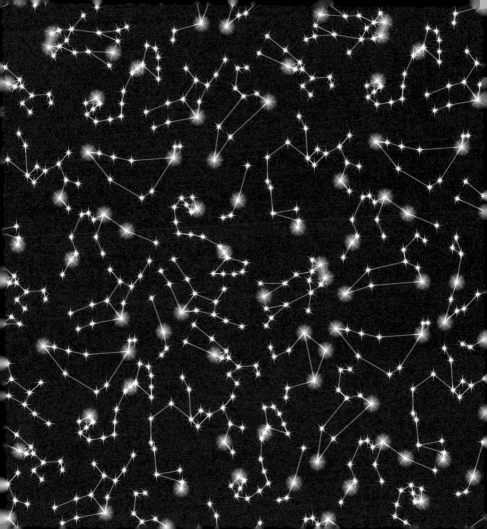

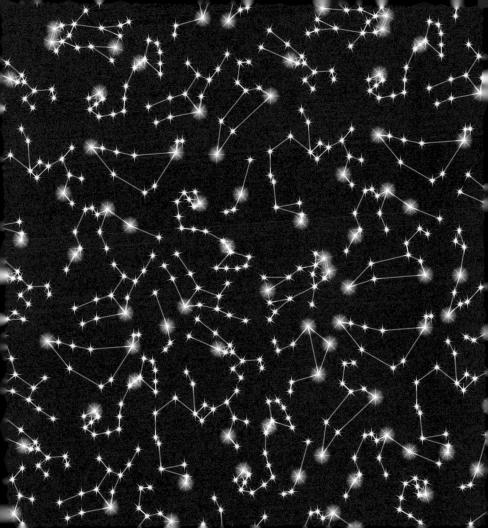

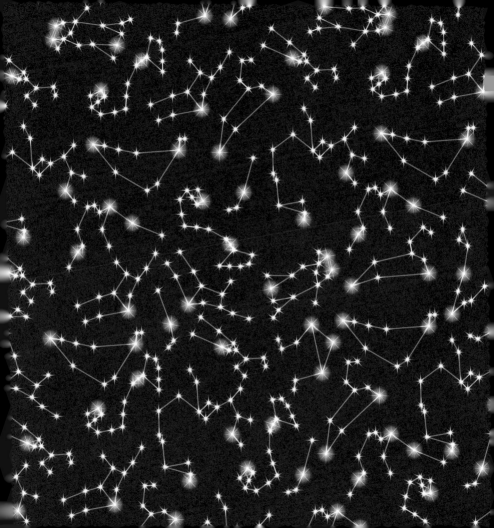

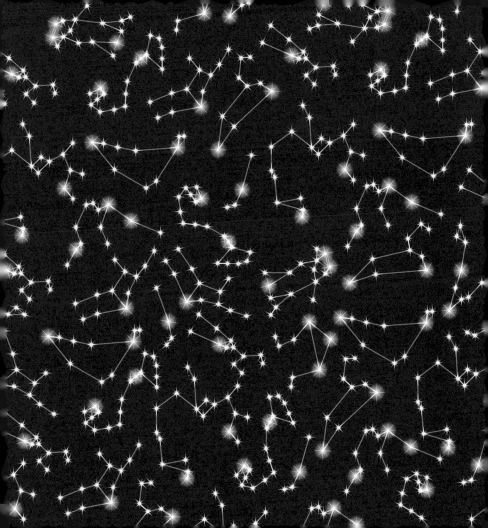

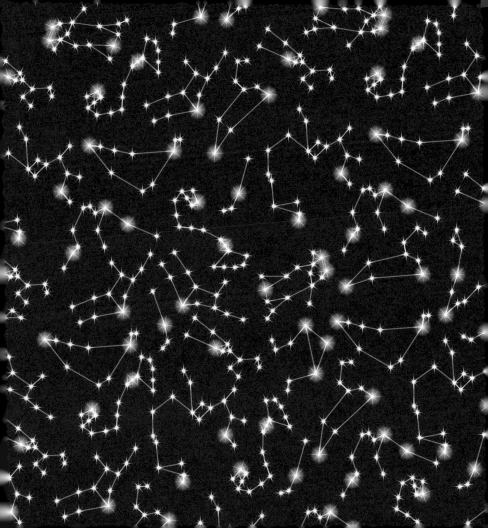

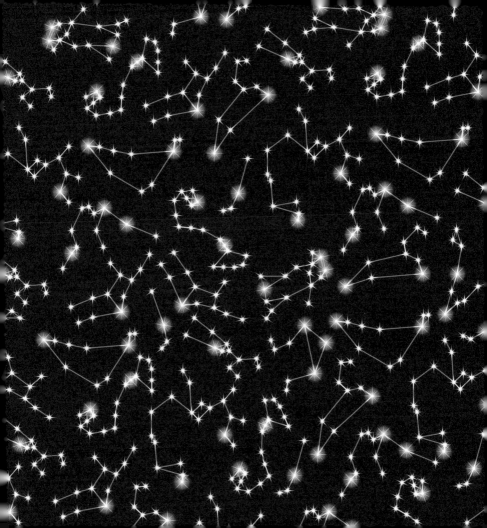

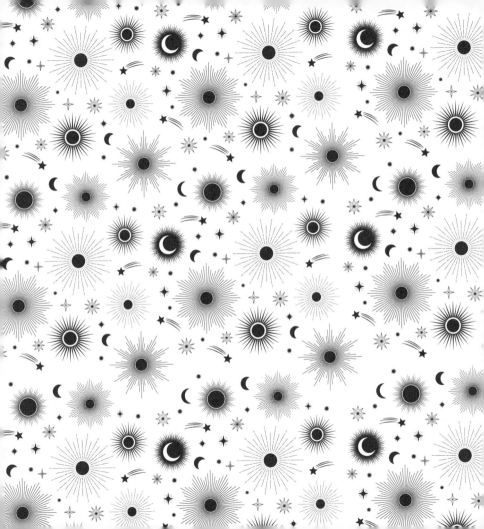

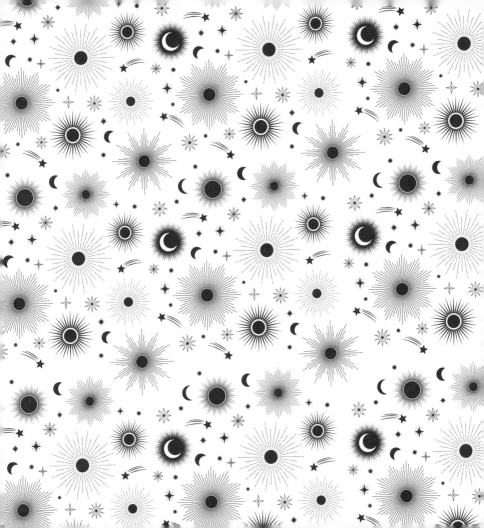